WEST CHICAGO PUBLIC LIBRARY DISTRICT

3 6653 00214 3612

2/12

D1190111

West Chicago Public Library District
118 West Washington
West Chicago, IL 60185-2803
Phone # (630) 231-1552
Fax # (630) 231-1709

KILLER SNAKES

Alex Woolf

ARCTURUS

This edition first published in 2011 by Arcturus Publishing

Distributed by Black Rabbit Books
P.O. Box 3263
Mankato
Minnesota MN 56002

Copyright © 2011 Arcturus Publishing Limited

Printed in China

All rights reserved.

Library of Congress Cataloging-in-Publication Data

Woolf, Alex, 1964-
 Killer snakes / Alex Woolf.
    p. cm. -- (Animal attack)
 Includes index.
 ISBN 978-1-84837-949-7 (library binding)
1. Snakes--Juvenile literature. 2. Poisonous snakes--Juvenile literature. 3. Dangerous reptiles--Juvenile literature. I.
Title.
 QL666.O6W64 2012
 597.96--dc22
                              2011006627

The right of Alex Woolf to be identified as the author of this work has been asserted by him in accordance with the
Copyright, Designs and Patents Act 1988.

Series concept: Alex Woolf
Editor and picture researcher: Alex Woolf
Designer: Ian Winton
Cover designer: Peter Ridley

Picture credits
Danleo: 15.
Nature Picture Library: 7 (Michael Richards/John Downer), 8 (Barry Mansell), 11 (Robert Valentic), 12 (Georgette
Douwma), 13 (Jurgen Freund), 14 (Rod Williams), 17 (Robert Valentic), 18 (Pete Oxford), 20 (Michael D. Kern), 22
(Tony Phelps), 23 (Robert Valentic), 25 bottom (Mary McDonald).
Photos.com: 26, 27 bottom.
Shutterstock: cover (Audrey Snider-Bell), 4 (Eric Isselée), 5 top (erlire74), 5 bottom (fivespots), 6 (EcoPrint), 9 top (Dr.
Morley Read), 9 bottom (Jason Mintzer), 10 (fivespots), 21 top (Maria Dryfhout), 21 bottom (AZPworldwide), 24 (Eric
Isselée), 25 top (Hannamariah), 27 top (Colette3), 28 (Brad Thompson).
Tigerpython: 29 bottom.
Warby, William: 19.
XLerate: 16.

Every attempt has been made to clear copyright. Should there be any inadvertent omission, please apply to the
publisher for rectification.

Supplier 03, Date 0411, Print Run 1045
SL001710US

Contents

S-ssskillful Hunters

Snakes are nature's ultimate "stealth" predators—sneaking up silently on their prey before striking with swift and deadly precision.

This is a rat snake, which is a constrictor, meaning that it kills its prey by crushing it.

Unlike their near relation, the lizard, snakes have no legs, and they must use their long, muscular, flexible bodies both for movement and to hold their prey.

SNACK ON THIS!

Snakes use their forked tongues to smell their prey. They also have ears-inside their bodies! Some even have organs in their upper lip that allow them to "see" the heat given off by their prey.

This snake is eating a mouse. Snakes do not chew their food. Their flexible jaws allow them to swallow their prey whole. Large snakes can open their jaws so wide, they can even swallow pigs!

Snake facts

- **Prey:** Small animals, including lizards, mammals, birds, eggs, fish, snails, insects, and other snakes
- **Tools:** Sense of smell, speed, venom-injecting fangs, constriction
- **Hunting methods:** Ambush and surprise attack

This is a temple pit viper. It kills by injecting its prey with venom.

Cobras

Cobras are famous for their hoods, which they inflate when angry or about to attack. They are also the only snakes in the world that build a nest for their young—just like birds, but on the ground!

There are 12 species of cobra. The biggest of these—the king cobra—is the largest venomous snake in the world.

The cape cobra lives in Southern Africa and can grow up to six feet. It can be aggressive, and its venom is powerful enough to kill a human within two to five hours of being bitten.

SNACK ON THIS!

Cobras inject so much venom in a single bite, they can kill an elephant.

As well as a strong sense of smell, cobras have excellent vision, and can even see in the dark. They can also sense tiny changes in temperature, which helps them to track their prey at night.

Spitting cobras are the only snake in the world that can spit their venom. They aim the venom at the eyes of their victims and are accurate to about half their own length!

Cobra facts

- **Length:** Varies from 4 to 18 feet
- **Lives in:** Southern Asia and Africa
- **Eats:** Birds, fish, frogs, lizards, eggs, chicks, other snakes

Coral Snakes

Coral snakes are shy creatures. They rarely bite humans, but when they do, the venom paralyzes the breathing muscles and is usually fatal.

Coral snakes are small, brilliantly colored and highly venomous. Most live in underground burrows or in piles of logs or rotting leaves. A few aquatic species of coral snake live in lakes and rivers.

SNACK ON THIS!

When threatened, the coral snake often curls the tip of its tail. This confuses the attacker as to which end is its head.

The coral snake delivers its venom through a pair of small fangs in the front of its top jaw. Unlike other venomous snakes, it tends to hold onto the victim while biting, giving time for the venom to take effect.

This variety, known as Hemprich's coral snake (above), is found in South America.

Coral snake facts

- **Length:** 1.6–5 ft.
- **Lives in:** Southern United States, Central and South America, Asia, Africa, Australia
- **Eats:** Smaller snakes, lizards, frogs, nesting birds, rodents

This harmless scarlet kingsnake mimics venomous coral snakes to deter predators from attacking. Locals learn to distinguish between the two with a rhyme: red to yellow, kill a fellow; red to black, venom lack.

Death Adders

The death adder is a highly venomous snake that lurks in the forests and wetlands of eastern and south-western Australia.

This snake has a curious method of hunting: it buries itself in the earth, leaving just its head and tail tip exposed. Then it wiggles its tail so it looks like a grub or worm—a tempting snack for any passing bird or mammal. When the unsuspecting animal approaches, the death adder strikes.

Death adders scent their prey by flicking their tongues in and out.

SNACK ON THIS!

The death adder has the fastest striking action of any snake. It can move from strike position to bite, then back to strike position in 0.13 seconds–the blink of an eye.

Death adders are very dangerous to humans because of their habit of lying very still and half buried. Unlike other snakes, they won't retreat at the approach of a human. A misplaced footfall can lead to a swift strike, and death in as little as six hours.

Death adders have thin, often brightly colored tail tips, which they use as a lure to attract their prey.

CHEW ON THAT!

Death adders are not actually adders! They belong to the elapid family, whereas adders are vipers. They are short and muscular with triangular heads, like adders, which may be how they got their name.

Sea Kraits

Sea kraits have blue or gray and black bands.

Not all snakes are land-based. Some, such as the sea krait, make their home in the sea. In fact, sea kraits are amphibious. They spend most of their lives in the ocean, but come ashore to rest or lay their eggs.

Sea krait facts

- **Length:** 3.3-5 ft.
- **Lives in:** Warm, tropical waters in the Pacific and Indian oceans
- **Eats:** Eels and small fish

Sea kraits look much like land snakes, but they have a few features that are useful for a life in the sea. These include a broad, paddle-like tail, flaps that close their nostrils while they are underwater, and a lung that extends almost the entire length of their body.

Sea kraits are venomous snakes. They usually hunt at night in the shallow seas around coral reefs and islands. They rarely attack people, although fishermen occasionally get bitten while sorting through a catch in their nets.

Sea kraits are excellent swimmers, found at depths ranging from 3 to 30 feet.

SNACK ON THIS!

Sea krait venom can be up to ten times as strong as rattlesnake venom. Luckily for swimmers, they have short fangs and are usually quite shy.

Mambas

There are two main kinds of mamba: green and black. Green mambas are fairly docile, tree-dwelling snakes. However, black mambas are aggressive, fast-moving land snakes.

The black mamba is actually gray in color—it gets its name from the black interior of its mouth.

SNACK ON THIS!

The black mamba is the fastest snake in the world, slithering along at speeds of up to 12 miles per hour.

The black mamba is one of the most feared snakes in Africa. There are stories that it will chase and attack humans, though there is no evidence of this. But if the mamba feels threatened, it will often attack repeatedly.

The black mamba is the longest venomous snake in Africa. The venom, injected through its fangs, attacks the heart and nervous system of its victims. One bite can easily kill a human.

Mamba facts

- **Length:** Black mambas average 8 ft., but can grow to 15 ft.
- **Lives in:** Western, southern, and eastern Africa
- **Eats:** Lizards, birds, rodents, and small mammals

The western green mamba is a native of the West African rain forest. Its venom is as toxic as the black mamba's, but the amount injected is less, due to the snake's smaller size.

Taipans

There are three known species of taipan: coastal, Central Ranges, and inland. Of these, the inland taipan, also known as the fierce snake, is the most dangerous. In fact, it is the most venomous land snake on earth. Its venom is 50 times deadlier than a cobra's and could kill an adult human in 45 minutes.

The inland taipan lives in the hot, dry parts of Central Australia. It hunts in the mornings and evenings when the desert is cooler.

SNACK ON THIS!

The inland taipan changes color through the seasons. It becomes darker in winter so that it can absorb more light and remain warm.

Taipan facts

- **Length:** 6-8.2 ft.
- **Lives in:** Australia and Papua New Guinea
- **Eats:** Birds, lizards, rats, mice, and bandicoots

Inland taipan snakes hatching. Female taipans lay up to 24 eggs at a time, and the eggs hatch two months later.

The taipan has excellent senses of smell and vision. When it finds its prey, it moves in very suddenly for the kill.

With small prey it bites and holds on, but with larger, more dangerous prey it bites, then retreats and waits for the poison to take effect.

Boomslangs

Boomslang means "tree snake" in Afrikaans, which is a good name for this highly venomous serpent, as it spends most of its life gliding through branches in African woods and forests.

The boomslang has a clever camouflage trick. It wraps most of its body around a branch, leaving just its front part sticking up straight like a twig. It can stay motionless in this position for hours, waiting for a bird or chameleon to come within range.

A boomslang remains stiff and motionless as it waits for its prey.

SNACK ON THIS!

The boomslang's eyes are among the largest (relative to head size) of any snake species.

This snake is agile and fast-moving. It strikes at its prey without warning, releasing a highly toxic venom through a set of fangs at the rear of its mouth.

Male boomslangs, like this one, tend to be bright green, with black or dark blue outlines to their scales. Females are a more muted, olive-brown color.

The venom stops blood from clotting, causing victims to die of internal and external bleeding. It is shy of humans, but has been known to bite when it feels threatened.

Boomslang facts

- **Length:** 3.3–5.3 ft.
- **Lives in:** Sub-Saharan Africa
- **Eats:** Tree-dwelling lizards, frogs, birds, and birds' eggs

Rattlesnakes

The rattlesnake gets its name from the rattle at the tip of its tail, which it shakes as a warning if it feels threatened.

The rattle is made up of hollow beads that click together when the tail is vibrated. The sound has been compared to the crackling sound of frying fat.

Of the many kinds of rattlesnakes, the most famous is the western diamondback, which is responsible for more attacks on humans than any other American snake—although their bites are rarely fatal.

SNACK ON THIS!

Rattlesnakes have two pits under their nostrils to detect the heat given off by warm-blooded prey. The pits are so sensitive, the snake can work out the exact size and location of the animal.

Rattlesnakes can inject different amounts of venom through their hollow fangs, depending on the size of the prey. The venom not only stuns the prey, but also starts the digestive process by breaking down the animal's tissue.

Before striking, rattlesnakes are coiled except for the front of their bodies, which is raised, and the rattle, which is buzzing. They can strike up to two thirds of their body length.

Rattlesnake facts

- **Length:** 3.3–5 ft. on average
- **Lives in:** Southwestern United States
- **Eats:** Mice, rats, ground squirrels, rabbits, lizards

The sidewinder rattlesnake gets its name from its unusual sideways method of moving across the desert sand.

Saw-Scaled Vipers

The saw-scaled viper may be small and rather ordinary-looking, but it is one of the most dangerous snakes in the world, responsible for many human deaths each year. The reasons for this are its choice of habitat (close to human settlements), highly toxic venom, and extreme aggression.

The snake usually hunts at night, moving around in a sidewinder fashion, or else half burying itself in readiness for an ambush.

The saw-scaled viper has large eyes with vertical pupils. This helps it to see well in dim light, which is useful for night hunting.

SNACK ON THIS!

Saw-scaled viper venom is used in the manufacture of a drug to prevent blood from clotting.

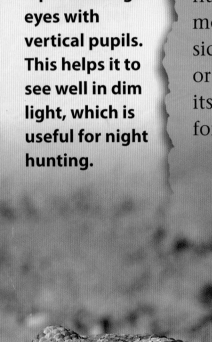

Saw-scaled viper facts

- **Length:** 15-24 in.
- **Lives in:** Indian subcontinent, Middle East, Central Asia
- **Eats:** Rodents, lizards, frogs, scorpions, centipedes and large insects

The brown, black, and gray patterns on the saw-scaled viper's back give it good camouflage.

The saw-scaled viper gets its name from its threat display. It forms its body into a series of tight loops and rubs them together to make a rasping, sizzling sound. This is usually the prelude to an attack from this easily angered snake.

Boas

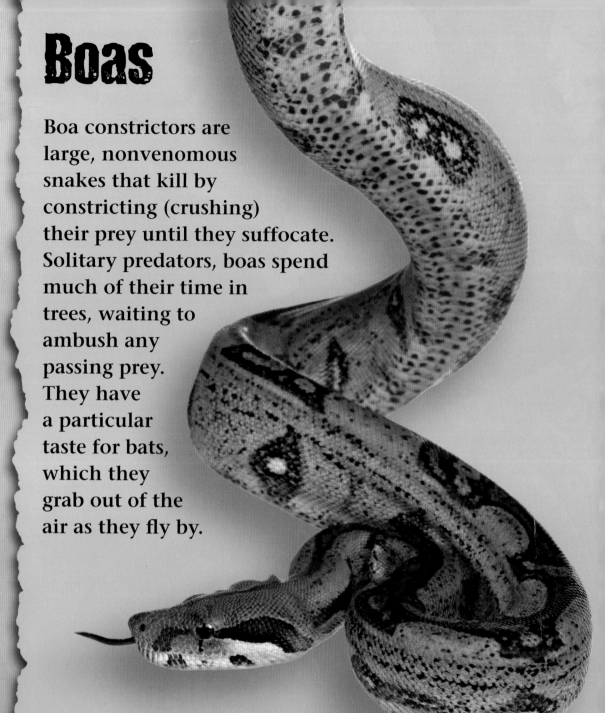

Boa constrictors are large, nonvenomous snakes that kill by constricting (crushing) their prey until they suffocate. Solitary predators, boas spend much of their time in trees, waiting to ambush any passing prey. They have a particular taste for bats, which they grab out of the air as they fly by.

Boas are covered with cream, brown, gray, and black oval and diamond patterns.

SNACK ON THIS!

Around 2 feet long at birth, boas grow continually throughout their 25- to 30-year lifespan.

Boas use heat sensors in their lips to locate warm-blooded prey. They have small, hooked teeth for grabbing and holding their victims while they wrap their coils around them and start to squeeze. It can take a boa six days to digest larger prey, after which it may not need to eat again for several months.

The emerald tree boa lives its life coiled over tree branches in the Amazon rain forest. At night it will drop its head downward and wait for prey to pass beneath.

Boa facts

- **Length:** 3-13 ft.
- **Lives in:** Rain forests, savannahs, and semiarid parts of Central and South America
- **Eats:** Rodents, lizards, mice, birds, bats, monkeys, wild pigs

A garden tree boa constricts a bat.

Anacondas

Anacondas are part of the boa family and are among the world's largest snakes. They are aquatic and live in and around the swamps and rivers of tropical South America. Like other boas, anacondas are constrictors— they kill their prey by crushing them to death in their coils.

The green anaconda's dark green and black scales give it excellent camouflage in its swampy habitat.

SNACK ON THIS!

The green anaconda competes with the reticulated python for the title of world's largest snake. Although the longest recorded python (33 ft.) beats the record-holding anaconda (28 ft.), the anaconda is far wider.

The anaconda hunts by night, feeding on fish, river fowl, caimans, and mammals. It is an ambush predator, biting its prey and then enveloping the animal in its coils, squeezing until it suffocates. It then swallows its victim whole.

(*Right*) Like the crocodile, the anaconda's nostrils are on top of its snout so it can breathe easily while swimming.

CHEW ON THAT!

Anacondas can eat enormous animals, such as alligators and deer. Like all snakes, they have a special, flexible jaw that opens very wide, so they can swallow their prey whole. It can take several weeks to digest very large prey.

A yellow anaconda swims along a shallow river.

27

Pythons

Pythons are large constrictor snakes dwelling in tropical and subtropical Asia, Africa and Australia.

Green tree pythons have vivid green scales to camouflage them against the rain forest canopy where they live and hunt.

SNACK ON THIS!

The world record for longest snake is held by a reticulated python killed in Celebes, Indonesia, in 1912. It measured exactly 33 feet.

Pythons are very adaptable. They enjoy both wet and dry conditions and can swim and climb trees, increasing the number of potential prey. Their color can be bright green or dull brown, depending on what camouflages them best in their particular habitat.

Pythons, like boas, are ambush predators, remaining motionless in camouflaged positions before striking suddenly at passing prey. The largest of them have been known to eat pigs, deer, and, occasionally, even children!

A baby python emerges from its shell. Unlike boas, which bear live young, female pythons lay eggs. They keep the eggs warm by causing their muscles to shiver, raising their own body temperature.

CHEW ON THAT!

Since the 1990s, wild pythons have been thriving in the Florida Everglades after some captive specimens escaped there and began breeding.

Glossary

agile Able to move quickly and easily.

ambush Launch a surprise attack from a concealed position.

amphibious Able to live both on land and in water.

aquatic Dwelling in or near water.

caiman A member of the alligator family native to South America.

camouflage An animal's natural colouring or form that enables it to blend in with its surroundings.

chameleon A type of lizard distinctive for its separately mobile eyes, elaborate crests, and for the ability of some types to change color so as to blend into its background.

constrictor A type of snake that kills its prey by constriction—crushing.

clotting (of blood) Forming into clots; thickening.

docile Peaceful; not aggressive.

elapid A family of venomous snakes that includes death adders, cobras, kraits, and mambas.

habitat A creature's natural environment.

lure Something used to tempt a person or animal to approach.

organ A part of the body that performs a particular function.

mimic Imitate or copy.

paralyse Cause a person or animal to become partly or wholly incapable of movement.

predator An animal that preys on other animals.

prey An animal that is hunted and killed by another animal for food.

rain forest Lush, dense forest, rich in diverse life forms, found mostly in tropical areas with heavy rainfall.

reticulated Like a network or grid. The reticulated python is so called because of the complex, gridlike pattern on its skin.

sensor An organ or device that detects things.

serpent Another word for snake.

solitary Living alone.

stealth Cautious, quiet movement.

suffocate Cause to die from lack of air.

threat display A form of behavior exhibited by some animals that is intended to scare away a potential enemy.

toxic Poisonous; harmful.

venom Poisonous fluid injected by some predators into their prey.

viper A family of venomous snakes that includes adders, saw-scaled vipers, and rattlesnakes.

Further Information

Books

Fun Facts About Snakes! by Carmen Bredeson (Enslow, 2009)

National Geographic Readers: Snakes! by Melissa Stewart (National Geographic, 2009)

Snakes by Louisa Somerville (Brown Bear, 2009)

Snakes by Seymour Simon (HarperCollins, 2007)

Time for Kids: Snake! by Lisa Jo Rudy (HarperCollins, 2005)

Venomous Snakes by Tim Harris (Gareth Stevens Publishing, 2010)

Web Sites

animals.howstuffworks.com/reptile/snake.htm
  Explains the anatomy of snakes, and how they live, move, eat, and reproduce.

www.bbc.co.uk/nature/order/Squamata
  All about snakes, lizards, and related species, including some spectacular images.

www.kidzone.ws/lw/snakes/index.htm
  Simple facts about snakes, including photos and activities.

www.reptileknowledge.com
  Contains lots of information about snakes and other reptiles.

www.venomoussnakes.net
  Information about the world's most dangerous snakes.

Index